SIMPLE FLOWERS

Arrangements
and
Floral Accents
for
the Home

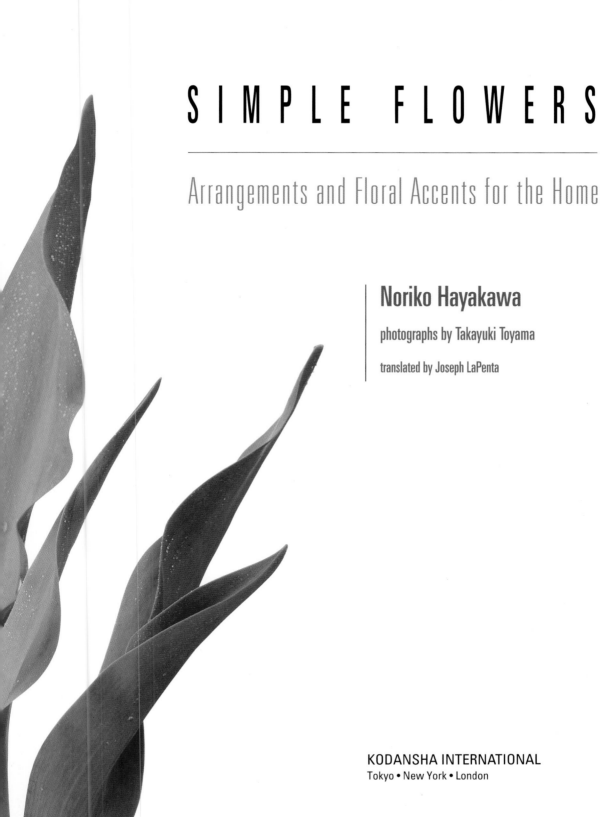

SIMPLE FLOWERS

Arrangements and Floral Accents for the Home

Noriko Hayakawa

photographs by Takayuki Toyama

translated by Joseph LaPenta

KODANSHA INTERNATIONAL
Tokyo • New York • London

CONTENTS

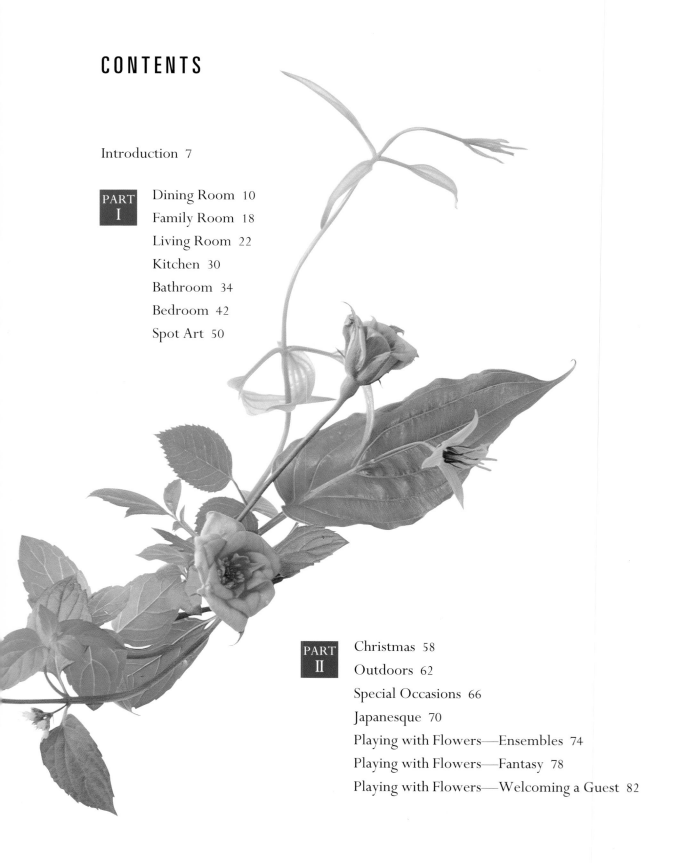

Illustrations on pages 106 to 108 by Tadamitsu Omori.

Published by Kodansha International Ltd., 17-14 Otowa 1-chome, Bunkyo-ku, Tokyo 112-8652, and Kodansha America, Inc.

Distributed in the United States by Kodansha America, Inc., 575 Lexington Avenue, New York, New York 10022, and in the United Kingdom and continental Europe by Kodansha Europe Ltd., 95 Aldwych, London WC2B 4JF.

ISBN 4-7700-2392-8

PART
I

Iris Centerpiece

Setting

A dining room table

Materials

① Rabbit-ear iris

② Dogwood

③ Bulrush/zebra bulrush

Comments

While it is possible to use a grouping of small flowers on a large table to give the effect of volume, here I chose to use a few impressive large flowers. Flowering branches of dogwood stretch into the surrounding space, integrating the arrangement with its setting. The irises stand boldly upright, and the bent strands of bulrush add charm and variation to this early summer arrangement.

Container

Because of the volume and scale of this work, I used a heavy ceramic pot and applied weights to the floral foam set inside it. The blue-and-white container proves a perfect match for the colors of the arrangement.

Variations

When arranging a collection of small flowers in this type of setting, you can use wine glasses like the ones shown here. Line up a number of glasses in the center of the table at irregular intervals and link them with a green, vinelike material such as ivy or smilax to create a sense of volume. Next, add many small flowers facing in all directions to make a diminutive but brilliantly colored arrangement. (See pages 94–101 for more details on small-container arrangements.)

Flowers in Tandem

Setting

A corner shelf or table

Materials

BOTTLE: ① Flowering indigo ② Spindle tree sprig
③ Carex grass
CUP: ④ Toad lily

Comments

My basic approach for corner arrangements is to follow an "L" pattern. In this two-vessel arrangement, the
vertical stroke of the "L" encompasses the flowers and
the bottle, while the horizontal movement extends from
the bottle's base to the small cup. I placed the bottle
and cup in the center of a corner shelf with an eye toward
balance and flow. Since a single container would floun-
der in this space, I chose to line up two containers of
different heights. I arranged a sprig of spindle tree in
the ceramic saké bottle to foster movement, its place-
ment stressing the line of the cutting and the fall colors
of the leaves. The other elements are more restrained
both in color and strength. In the shallow saké cup, a
single toad lily rests in a calm, natural manner.

Container

While I used a ceramic saké bottle and cup here, any
number of everyday objects would be equally effective.
Simple, casual containers work well with wildflowers,
and show off their gentle qualities. Arrangements using
multiple containers arrayed in a single space should have
some elements in common—color, shape, materials—
to give the whole work a sense of unity and harmony.

Variations

You might try placing a rectangular piece of cloth in
the center of a shelf and then setting a tall flower vase
on top of it and slightly off-center to the left. In the
vase, arrange plants like ivy or rosemary, with their
curving lines flowing into the space on the right.

Table Centerpiece in Natural Tones

Setting

A dining room table

Materials

① Beauty berry ② Vine carrot with flowers
③ Evergreen fern

Comments

Keep arrangements for the dining room table simple—not too tall or too large. Nothing should interfere with the progress of the meal or the pleasure of
the diners. I used a clipping of vine carrot, with its
white-and-purple flowers, to echo the left-right movement of the table and chose flowers and berries with
complementary colors for a more natural effect. As a
basic guide, the volume of a centerpiece should be less
than one-third the width of the table, and no taller than
the length spanning elbow and wrist.

Container

The mat and bowl are of recycled paper, and their
quiet tones work well with the soft natural feel of the
simple wooden table.

Variations

Brownish or beige pottery would also be appropriate here.

Flowers & Berries on a Tray

Setting

A wooden tray on a low glass table

Materials

① Cornflower

② Grapevine with unripe grapes

Comments

This is just an ordinary wine glass, but add two or three flowers to it and the setting acquires a calm, intimate atmosphere. With such a small receptacle, simplicity is the key. Limiting the types of materials works best with mini-arrangements. But as a floral design with a single material soon becomes monotonous, I varied the lengths of the stems and faced each flower in a different direction to break the pattern and create interest. While working to achieve the right balance and expression, pay careful attention not only to each cutting's natural irregularities but to the space between the flowers. Heighten the seasonal feeling of the tray by placing fruit, vines, and dry leaves on or around the tray or table in a casual manner.

Container

Small flowers placed on this kind of tray tend to assert themselves very strongly. Make sure to match the color and material of the tray to the type of flowers and the setting.

Variations

For a glass table, small, light containers encourage a relaxed feeling. You can also use wildflowers in baskets woven from vines, inserting a small glass to hold the water.

Vase of Autumn Colors

Setting

A small end table

Materials

① Calla lily   ② "Chocolate" cosmos

③ Asparagus fern   ④ Evergreen fern

Comments

With an arrangement in a glass container, you should take special care with the part that is visible inside the glass. A beautiful arrangement can be spoiled by a crowded, confused mass of leaves and stems below. Instead of floral foam or a needlepoint holder, you can place individual leaves in the water to secure materials, but keep in mind that you must position the leaves for functional as well as aesthetic appeal.

For this grouping, I chose to emphasize the graceful lines of the cosmos stems while making sure they were not parallel. Because the chocolate color is so rich and deep, cutting the stem too short would spoil the flower's

strength and striking presence. The colors of the phone stand, the vessel, and the plants harmonize beautifully in this very simple work.

Variations

A blue or green porcelain vase with blue belladonna and white roses, coupled with any green material that has an interesting sense of motion, would work well in this space. If the container you select does not match the setting as well as you would like, place it on a lace doily, cloth, or small tray.

mple Greenery

Setting

throom windowsill

Materials

ler plant ② Isotoma

③–④ Greenery
) Broom ④ Fennel)

Comments

t on the windowsill of a bathroom
en greenery without flowers has a
though a soft second color adds a
chantment. I selected green leaves
ain materials, and created variety
gs with different shapes and leaf
our species, including vines, two-
l specimens with variegated leaves.

ity and is commonly associated with colors like white,
green, and blue, and transparent materials like glass.
If you do use a glass or ceramic container, it should
be low and stable and set in a place where it will not
interfere with everyday activities.

Container

bathroom must be selected with
eanliness is the most important qual-

Variations

Arrangements of white or small blue flowers would
look lovely by themselves.

throom Bouquet

Setting

ed grouping set into the side of
a bathroom sink

Materials

e ② Small sunflower

oke tree ④ Rosemary

Comments

lowers should not be too tall. Your
be low-lying and natural. You will
enough space around the faucet in
re with the daily usage of the sink.
curvature the basin, you could try
oral foam to the side as I did here,
astic pin holder secured with floral
he entrance is on the left, the toilet to
ors suggest the direction from which
seen and should look their best.

Container

Since space is limited in this kind of arrangement,
floral foam substitutes for a flower vase.

Variations

The color of the flowers should complement the tones
of the walls or the tiles. Flowers with beautiful fra-
grances—such as freesia, hyacinth, and stock—are also
very effective here.

41

A sense of calm intimacy should be the keynote of arrangements for the bedroom. Simple flowers that harmonize with mirrors, figurines, photographs, and other personal accessories work much better than large, independent, showy arrangements.

Bedside Bouquet

Setting

A bedside table

Materials

① Lapeirousa

② Buttercup

③ Euonymus

Comments

A petite arrangement of flowers on a bedside table has a peaceful, calming effect. My basic approach is to use small, light flowers that harmonize with the pattern and color of the container and have a subtle fragrance. Avoid heavy flowers and those with thick stems that have a tendency to fall over even if wire is used to secure them, as was done here.

Container

Familiar objects like teacups make appropriate containers for small flowers, and using a saucer gives a sense of stability suitable for a bedside table. Since the arrangement will be seen by someone lying in bed, avoid tall containers. To secure the materials, roll up some wire and hang it on the rim of the cup, then insert the flowers in the rolled wire.

Variations

The kinds and colors of cups are various, and the ways they can be combined with small flowers are infinites. Take a look at your collection of teacups with an eye toward mini-arrangements. The secret is to combine the cup and the plants in an artful way. For more details see Arranging with Teacups, pages 94–97.

Angel's Wreath

A bureau or chest

Materials

① Miniature rose ② Kiwi vine

③ Spearmint ④ Silver brunia

⑤ English ivy

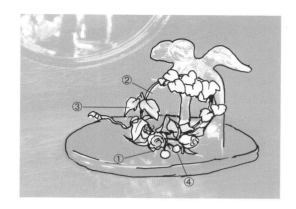

Comments

This tiny wreath is made of kiwi vine left over from the full-sized wreath shown on page 59. As "recycled" material, the display life is limited. However, reusing flowers from previous arrangements after removing wilted foliage is a technique that deserves more attention.

Here, I set the clippings on a stand in a design reminiscent of their first incarnation. The flowers and leaves are tied to the vine with very fine wire. While the life span of this arrangement will be shorter still in this waterless setting, the wreath took on a real sense of presence when I placed it against a small glass angel, making the effort worthwhile. To flesh out the arrangement, I added some new material.

Breaking with Form

Setting

A bureau or chest

Materials

① Amsonia ② Meadowsweet
③ Winter hazel

Comments

An irregular shape among the sturdy rectangular forms of a formal setting brings a spark of variety and life. Think of the vessel and the flowers as new, if temporary, elements of the entire space. Place the container so that it does not interfere with the picture on the wall, and is well situated in regard to the photographs. An asymmetrical receptacle like this teapot is a challenging choice for spaces without a central focus. The handle and spout are interesting features and should not be covered. I arranged the materials tall on the right and flowing out to the left side, choosing the blue wildflowers with the color of the container in mind. I added small, white spirea to bring out the color of the pale blue amsonia.

Container

The arrangement plays on the individual characteristics of this large, ceramic teapot, with the clippings arranged to create a sense of movement.

Variations

Depending on the space, you could try a tandem arrangement as on page 15: place a teacup in the space to the left of the pot and make a small, low arrangement in it of the same materials used in the pot, following the hints given in Arranging with Teacups, pages 94–97.

Bedrooms are usually done in restful, low-keyed colors, and cool arrangements can deepen the tranquil mood. But bright flowers in unique containers can also work as delightful, refreshing counterpoints to a quiet ambiance.

In a Looking Glass

Setting

A bedroom bureau with mirror

Materials

① Tulip

② Adonis

③ Kalanchoe

Comments

Because of the doubling effect of the mirror, less looks like more so take care not to use too much material. When placed near heavy wooden furniture, robust-colored flowers work better than those with soft, pastel tones. Since the dominant color of both flowers and container is red you can create variation and sustain interest by using flowers of different sizes, shapes, and stages of bloom—closed, partially opened, and fully opened blossoms.

Container

I selected this vase because it complements the burgundy frame of the mirror. The deep red harmonizes with

the rather weighty interior colors. The arrangement should not be too tall otherwise it might obstruct the view in the mirror. By using a container with a narrow mouth and arranging the thick stems of the tulips first, the rest of the materials will be easier to secure in place.

Variations

Avoid using a whitish container in this setting. Try such large, intensely colored blooms as sunflowers, roses, or red or yellow lilies. Place them in luxurious lacquer containers with rich red or brown tones or other similar vessels with deep but muted tones.

Lively Corner

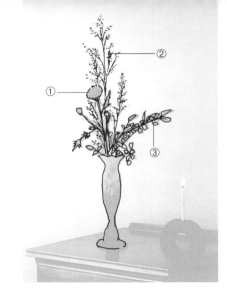

Setting

A corner side table

Materials

① Thistle ② Ruby grass

③ Blueberry

Comments

When working in a corner, you should pay special attention to the L-shape of the arrangement and its position in relation to the walls. Here, I also tried to make the most of the unique shape of this attractive vase by not hiding it with materials that cascade downward.

Container

This Art Nouveau–style vase has a narrow mouth, which makes it particularly suitable for confined spaces. Containers with wide mouths allow material to spread out too far, which upsets the overall balance of space and arrangement. You can get an even more natural effect by using a vase with a color that harmonizes with the table. For containers of less harmonious tones, set a mat, cloth, or tray with color tones that will bridge the difference between table and container.

Variations

I chose thistles to match the thistle motif of the vase, but a brilliantly colorful spray of autumn maple leaves would also work well with the form, color, and pattern of this vase. In a container with a narrow mouth, avoid using flowers with thick stems.

Spring Visitors

Setting

An unconventional container on a bedside table

Materials

① Amur adonis ② Fern shoot

③ Green barley

Comments

Generally, I would avoid a white container in this type of setting, but the vessel's unusual shape tempted me to try it. I chose small fern shoots for their oddly impressive postures, then added depth to the arrangement by placing the shoots at various heights and pointing them in different directions.

Container

Fern shoots have such a unique character that a strong, irregular container is more appropriate than one with delicate features.

Variations

Small but unusual flowers are effective here. Try round ones like thistles and globe amaranth, or oddly shaped plants like sweet pea and strawberry candle.

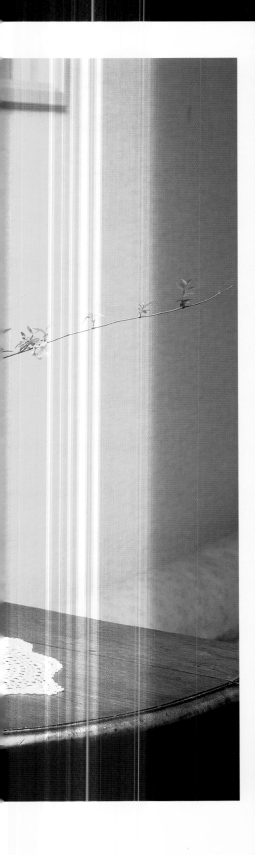

Flowers are excellent for enlivening unused nooks and crannies and other out-of-the-way spots,
where they make charming surprises for guests and family members alike. Such spaces
call for originality in the choice of materials and container.

Filling a Niche

Setting

A small niche with a classical framework

Materials

① Green briar with berries

② Orchid

③ Rosemary

④ Lawson cypress

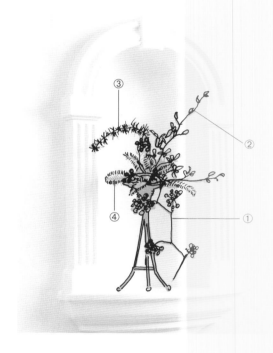

Comments

In this niche, which is tall but not very wide or deep, a tall vessel with a narrow mouth works well. I selected a stylish iron candleholder and red and green materials to suit the holiday season. Keeping the arrangement sparse on the left, right, and in the front, I stressed the height of the space by extending the flowers and branches in vertical lines, which emphasizes the gentle curves of the rosemary, the comfortably rising lines of the orchids, and the angular quality of the branches of green briar.

Variations

In spring, try soft, pastel flowers in a tall champagne glass. Light flowers with thin stems like pansies, lilies of the valley, or marguerites can be combined with bright green asparagus fern or smoke grass.

Around a Stairway

A small table in an auxiliary space

Materials

① Bletilla ② False goat's beard
③ Glossy abelia

Comments

I chose a pastel gray vase to go with the gray wall-paper. I used flowers with thin stems that slid easily into the narrow mouth of the vase, and tried to give the whole work a casual grace.

Container

In tall vases, an arrangement with a downward movement unifies the materials and the container, but it is difficult to create such a cascading arrangement when the mouth of the container is narrow. In this work at the foot of a staircase, I took advantage of the stability provided by the narrow mouth to arrange the materials with a strong rising movement that suits the space perfectly.

Variations

Using a container and flowers with warm color tones to match the table would also be effective here.

Green Cascade

Setting

A wall above an antique chest

Materials

①–③ Cascading greenery
(① Periwinkle ② Clematis ③ Others)

④ False anemone ⑤ Agrimony ⑥ Lotus leaf

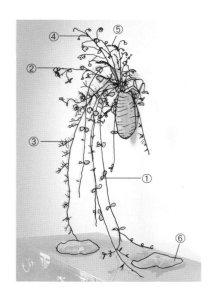

Comments

Arrangements hung from the wall should cascade downward. The higher the container is placed, the wider the space the arrangement will command. You can give an overall sense of rhythm to the work by using vines and stems of varying lengths that flow downward at slightly different angles.

Container

When selecting a vessel for a wall arrangement, avoid large, heavy, or unstable containers.

Variations

I chose flowers that face downward and other materials that emphasize a feeling of downward flow. For interesting variations, try lily of the valley, fritillary, star lily, and other lilies that seem to be nodding in the summer heat.

Approach spot arrangements with a sense of play. Try placing unconventional containers in unexpected places, and remember that the trick is to make the most of the natural characteristics of the materials, their colors, lines, and surfaces.

Hearth-Side Flowers

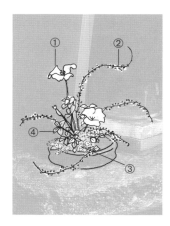

Setting

By the side of
a fireplace

Materials

① Glove tulip

② Thunberg spirea

③ Kohuhu

④ Lady's mantle

Comments

When not in use, the fireplace area can often be enlivened with a simple "spot arrangement." This warm spring grouping emphasizes the fine, soft curves of the spirea and focuses on the fresh yellow flowers in the center. I gave careful consideration to the movement of the spirea, then completed the base with bright green grasses. The thin stems of the tulips give the flowers their independence, and in this arrangement the yellow blooms take on the appearance of fluttering butterflies.

Container

I selected a shallow stone dish to go with the stone fireplace and used a needlepoint holder to secure the materials. Because the dish blends well with its surroundings, the small arrangement seems to float up into view.

Variations

A simple basket would work well here, or a container surrounded and hidden by bricks or logs. In either case, the dark background demands light flowers with a fresh feeling.

Folk Craft Elegance

Setting

A round wooden table

Materials

① Cherry sage

② Spearmint

③ English ivy

④ Pink-tinged leaf

Comments

I found this spice box, a common handmade article used in everyday life in southern India, at a folk-crafts bazaar, and I was immediately attracted by its warmth. It seemed a natural choice for arranging the herbs I had cultivated in my garden. The cherry sage and the pinkish-red leaves underscore the rich tones of the box and the setting. Keep the flowers light to make a bright, fresh impression and act as a counterbalance to the rather dark and heavy wood tones of the room and container.

Variations

With the cover opened wider, larger flowers like gerbera and small sunflowers would work well here, as would variegated pineapple mint leaves and flowers with a yellow color tone.

PART
II

CHRISTMAS

You need not stick to the customary Christmas colors: red, green, and white. Try subdued monochromatic arrangements with touches of gold or silver, or make your own personal variation of the traditional Christmas wreath.

Christmas Centerpiece

Setting

A dining room table

Materials

① Oregon fir

② Southern star

③ Miniature rose

④ Cape myrtle

⑤ Ornamental silver braid

Comments

I imagined a silver wintry world outside the window, and inside the welcoming flames of a fireplace crackling in the background. To a beautifully fragrant base of Oregon fir, I added simple white flowers. The mass of the arrangement expands to the left and right, echoing the shape of the table. The silver container, candles, and braid complement this low-key, refined centerpiece. Keep the arrangement low to avoid distraction during dining.

Variations

For a simple but creative arrangement, use many thin pink candles in a fir or pine base, and complete the work with two or three varieties of pink flowers, such as gerbera or wax flower. You might even consider adding some quiet pink ribbons.

A Window Scene

Setting

A simple Christmas arrangement on a window table

Materials

① Miniature rose

② Lawson cypress

Comments

Considering the view through the window, I placed a low container in front, and a taller one of a different shape and color behind it. The second container is in harmony with the first, and is used to add a sense of varia-tion. Both are of the same kind of glass, and each holds a single flower of the same color as the container. A branch of cypress placed on the table evokes the spirit of Christmas. Effective and simple.

A Different Kind of Wreath

Setting

A wreath for the front door or entrance hall

Materials

① Rose ② Kiwi vine

③ Leucadendron

④ Dusty miller

⑤–⑧ Light, airy greenery
(⑤ Grain stalk ⑥ Dog hobble/rainbow leaf
⑦ Gum tree ⑧ English ivy)

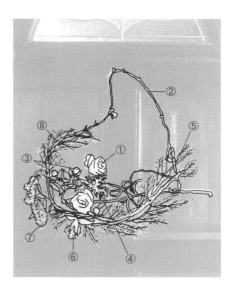

Comments

Kiwi vines have both thick and thin sections. As you acquire experience working with them—making cir-cular shapes, knotting and tying them—there will come a time when suddenly everything falls into place and very interesting forms emerge. Once you have the form you want, tie the vine firmly with wire at each of the most important points, and use more wire to secure a piece of floral foam to the vine. Since foam saturated with water is quite heavy, attach it so that the weight does not distort the shape of the wreath. If you hang the wreath up high, pay careful attention to the direction of the flowers, some of which should look down at the viewer. Emphasize the shape of the vine and avoid putting too much material outside the main line. You can also add an extra natural touch by twining ivy or other vinelike plants around the kiwi.

Variations

For Christmas, try gradations of green with pointlike accents of red roses. Combining two or more kinds of green, such as fir, cypress, or rosemary, will produce beautiful variations.

*Outdoor arrangements present special challenges. They must be bright and distinctive enough to stand
out against a natural setting, and stable enough to keep their form even when exposed to wind.*

Picnic Flowers

Setting

A picnic spread

Materials

① Small sunflower ② Violet foxtail
③ Umbrella fern ④ Begonia leaf

Comments

At a picnic on a sunny afternoon a cheerful bunch of
flowers can add immeasurably to your outing. So along
with the wine, bread, and cheese consider a simple bouquet. Bright flowers and those with a strong presence
can hold their own outdoors against a natural setting.

Here, the straight lines of the foxtail, which can be
found almost anywhere, offer a solid contrast to the
bushy, round forms of the sunflowers. With a simple
two-color arrangement, such variations in form are
very important. I used the sunflowers tall, and arranged
the other materials with thought given to their height
and direction. The foxtails rise above the sunflowers,
and green ferns and leaves are used sparingly at the
base of the arrangement.

Container

For a picnic, a common daily article like this pitcher
may work better than an expensive container. Out of
doors, an arrangement is subject to wind, so floral
foam is the safest choice for keeping the materials in
place. I put the foam inside the pitcher and created a flat,
stable surface for the arrangement by setting a board
under the tablecloth.

Variations

Instead of the pitcher, you can use a jam bottle or a can
with a decorative label. In spring, try a simple gather-
ing of tulips, arranging them to face in various directions
and adjusting the leafy cuttings between the flowers
effectively.

Welcoming Guests

Setting

Near the front entrance to a home

Materials

① Yellow cosmos

② Monkshood

③ Themeda grass

④–⑤ Greenery
(④ Japanese honeysuckle ⑤ Umbrella plant)

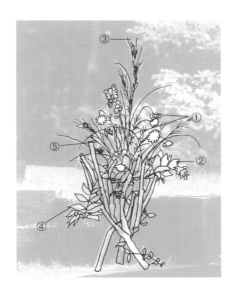

Comments

A stand fashioned from branches is perfect for this outdoor setting. I used floral foam in the rustic container nesting in the center of the branches because even a slight wind can cause the materials to shift. Starting with the simple color contrast between the two autumn flowers, cosmos and monkshood, I finished by incorporating grasses from the surrounding natural environment.

Variations

Try an outdoor arrangement in a container surrounded by stones, again using floral foam to anchor the grouping against the wind. Outdoor arrangements work best when composed of flowers in colors that offer a distinct contrast to the surroundings.

Borrowing Background

Setting

A verandah

Materials

① Japanese rose of Sharon   ② Viburnum

③ Knotgrass

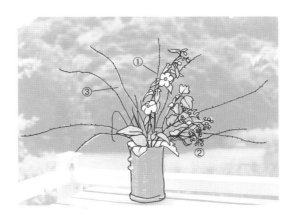

Comments

For this arrangement on a verandah, the deep surrounding greenery functions much as the background of a painting, filling out and creating a satisfying contrast to the basic red tones of this floral composition: the red of stems loaded with berries, the red centers of the flowers, and the thin, finely detailed red lines of the knotweed. I limited the materials and allowed the greenery in the background to complete the arrangement. In a sense, this is a contemporary version of a Japanese traditional gardening technique of "borrowed scenery" in which the surrounding environment is incorporated into the work.

Container

I selected a ceramic container that would go well against the green and blue vista, placing the vessel low enough to give an unobstructed view of the wooden handrail with all its natural warmth.

Variations

Taking advantage of a natural backdrop can contribute much to a work and is particularly striking when the mountains are ablaze with the fiery tints of autumn.

A Romantic Evening
An Afternoon Tête-à-Tête

SPECIAL OCCASIONS

Creating arrangements for a special evening or get together can be a sign of thoughtfulness, concern, or even intimacy. Just as you choose music, select flowers and vases to fit the occasion—whether it be romantic, festive, recalling shared memories, or renewing old friendships.

A Romantic Evening

Setting

A centerpiece for a glass table

Materials

① Tulip

② Lily of the valley

③ Fairy bell

④ Acacia

Comments

This spring arrangement would be perfect for a birthday, an Easter celebration, or a romantic evening for two. Lily of the valley is set firmly in a glass vase in the center. It is surrounded by eggshells used as containers for yellow tulips and acacia, which stretch to the left and right. For impact and simplicity, I confined the colors of this work to yellow and white.

Container

To use eggshells as containers, first make a tiny hole in the tapered end of an egg. Carefully increase the size of the opening, then empty out the contents and rinse the shell. Finally, adjust the size of the opening to the thickness of the flower stem you wish to insert.

Variations

Do not cover glass tables with pieces of cloth placed beneath arrangements. Instead, use a complementary glass container. For a refreshing summer arrangement, float hydrangeas in a glass bowl.

An Afternoon Tête-à-Tête

Setting

A light centerpiece on a kitchen or dining room table

Materials

① Marguerite

② Delphinium

③ Corn lily

④ Small lily leaf

Comments

The white and blue evoke a cool feeling. I placed floral foam in a blue glass bowl and surrounded it with glass marbles to keep it from floating to the surface. I deliberately selected flowers with thin, fine stems, and arranged them so that they stretch out from the center in all directions with gentle movements, like water flowing from a fountain.

Variations

These materials would work very well in a tall, compote-like container placed in the center of the table. However, for arrangements on a table where food or drink is served, avoid using flowers that shed pollen, or those with a strong scent.

JAPANESQUE

In the traditional Japanese art of ikebana, arranging flowers in standard vessels is just one approach. All kinds of objects—whether round, oblong, square; shallow, deep, or tall—can be enlisted to produce striking displays. The examples here and in the pages that follow should inspire you to take a fresh look at the everyday household articles around you that can be adapted for creative use.

Approaching Ikebana

Setting

An entrance hall, shelf, or stand

Materials

① Amaryllis

② Bittersweet with berries

③ Knotweed/jointweed

④ Knotgrass

Comments

Think of the entry hall as the "face" of your home, the first "room" guests see. Even a small arrangement of seasonal materials, such as this ikebana-inspired design, will make a lasting impression. Here, red is the main color tone, and the combination of the soft curves of knotweed with its tiny flowers and the strong lines of the bittersweet branches create a lively rhythmic contrast.

Container

Since branches loaded with berries are unstable when set upright and might easily topple even a large vase, use them mainly in a wide container and secure them firmly in place with a needlepoint holder.

Variations

A round or oval container is better suited to a semicircular surface than one with sharp corners. You can also use floral foam or needlepoint holders placed on opposite sides of a low bowl with a broad base, and add fragrant flowers like lilies or roses, keeping them low and close together.

A Touch of Lacquer

Setting

A shelf with a *shoji* paper-screen background

Materials

① Black lily

② Cymbidium

Comments

The stems of the two black lilies have very different postures, and for variation I arranged one tall and one low. Between them, I placed a single cymbidium flower. The leaves of the cymbidium flow out from the side opposite the flower. I chose the black lily, with its quiet presence, to harmonize with the tranquility of the room.

Container

The container is antique lacquer with a Chinese ambiance. Lacquerware is made to hold liquids, but some older pieces have cracked with age so to protect them you should cover the bottom with soft paper and place a small container inside to hold the water and arrangement.

Variations

Clematis or star lily would work fine here, as would a larger lacquer container.

Welcoming the New Year

Setting

An entrance hall

Materials

① Camellia   ② Pine   ③ Willow with leaf buds

Comments

For this rather formal arrangement in an assemblage of lacquered boxes to celebrate the New Year, I have used the traditional Japanese materials: pine, the symbol of long life; willow, which puts forth leaf buds at the turn of the year; and camellia, which is known as the monarch of winter flowers. I staggered the piled boxes, and arranged the straight branches of pine and the curving willow tall and with a nice sense of space between them. For contrast, the white camellias are placed low, while the red, braided cord provides a festive accent.

Container

Piling up the lacquered boxes, which are meant to hold special New Year's food, creates a dramatic effect. With this arrangement, I have tried for a dignified but simple beauty that would also highlight the resonance of the lacquerware.

Variations

Instead of camellias, a flower like amur adonis would also go well here, and plum branches (Japanese apricot) would liven up the atmosphere. For a more modern approach, use one box, fill it with water, and float red and white camellias on the surface.

Three Round Tables
Drinks & Hors d'Oeuvres

PLAYING WITH FLOWERS
—ENSEMBLES—

*Here are suggestions for ensemble arrangements using multiple containers and different but related groups
of flowers. The possibilities for group displays are endless. The secret is to take a flexible approach
and "orchestrate" arrays of receptacles, flowers, grasses, and leaves.*

Three Round Tables

Setting

Along a wall or fronting a terrace

Materials

LEFT

① Aster ② "Wild frosty"

CENTER

③ Clematis ④ Blueberry leaf

RIGHT

⑤ Rose ⑥ Clematis with seed

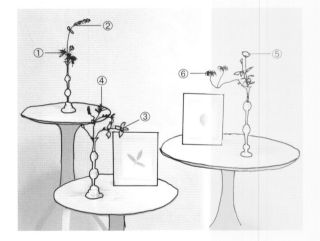

Comments

The typical approach to arrangements in large spaces is to use big containers and a massive amount of material. Here, I have taken the opposite approach, creating an ensemble of three mini-arrangements. I assembled a well-balanced array of tables of different heights, delicate glass containers, and arrangements that use only a few items per vase. Lovely flowers and grasses of the kind that bloom at the side of the road play the lead. Arrange them in a simple but stylized manner and make sure to vary the heights of the cuttings.

Drinks & Hors d'Oeuvres

Setting

A portable arrangement on a slab of cherry tree

Materials

FRONT

① Aster

② Toad lily (pink)

③ Leaves to cover

BACK

④ Persimmon branch with unripe fruit

⑤ Toad lily (yellow)

⑥ Sweet scabious

⑦ Leaves to cover

Comments

This kind of setting is perfect for a friendly get together over drinks and hors d'oeuvres. Here, the setting is exotic—featuring lilies with Japanese saké cups — but you could easily substitute small garden flowers to accompany glasses of wine, pre-dinner aperitifs, or an after-dinner brandy.

The slab of wood functions as a tray or table and can be placed wherever you like—indoors on a rug near the fireplace or outdoors on a patio table or bench.

The flower groupings should be small and unobtrusive. It is also important to consider not only the variations in color of each mini-arrangement but the spaces between them.

Container

I used cracks and holes in the surface of the wood to secure the flowers, but floral sponge firmly secured with floral tape and well hidden by leaves could also be used.

Unexpected Encounter

Silk & Flowers

Bamboo Forest

PLAYING WITH FLOWERS
—FANTASY—

Here are examples of arrangements that can please, amuse, or even shock the viewer much as a surrealist painting might do. With a little imagination, ordinary spaces can become unexpected settings for fantasy.

Unexpected Encounter

Setting

A tubular container on a stairway banister

Materials

① Spray chrysanthemum

② Corn cockle

③ Gentian

④ Millet

⑤ Laurel

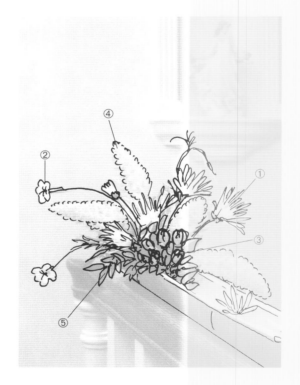

Comments

It is possible to enliven unlikely spaces such as this hallway with flowers. However, since people pass the banister rather quickly, I kept the whole arrangement low and developed a multisided composition that could be enjoyed from any direction.

Container

I chose cut bamboo for this long, narrow space, although other elongated objects could be used. Given the con-

fines of the space and the fact that people are constantly coming and going in the vicinity, the container had to be set firmly in place, so I tied the bamboo to the banister with a fine wire hidden by the arrangement.

Variations

It is also possible to use camellias or roses, placing them in a long container to look as if they are floating.

Silk & Flowers

Setting

A mantelpiece

Materials

① Prairie gentian   ② China aster   ③ Stemona

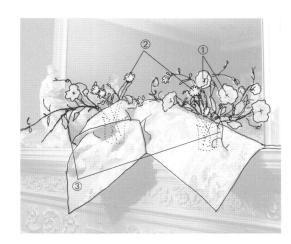

Comments

An arrangement in a long, narrow space like this one looks best when it has two or three focal points. I varied the scale, creating both large and small floral groupings to produce interesting modulated effects. I also paid particular attention to the mirror in the background, carefully considering the reflected view of the flowers as well.

Container

I used the silk *obi* sash of a kimono to hide two small cups that were not very interesting in themselves. Any narrow strip of beautiful cloth, folk textile, or even hand-made Japanese paper would work well in this kind of space.

Variations

Try an arrangement of wine glasses of different heights. With the doubling effect created by the mirror reflecting the flowers, you will need fewer materials than you might imagine. (See pages 98–101 for other examples of group arrangements in small glass containers.)

Bamboo Forest

Setting

A fireplace

Materials

① Hydrangea   ② Horse mint

③ Smoke grass   ④ Ground cover

Comments

In the warmer months, when it is not being used, a fireplace offers a challenging space to work in. You could simply place a vessel with an arrangement in the space, but I opted for a cluster of containers to create the impression of a vast bamboo grove rustling and swaying in a cool breeze. The point here is to evoke a natural setting on a small scale, much as a well-sculpted garden might.

Container

I used a number of quiet, tasteful pottery containers that harmonize well with the color and physical quality of the bamboo.

Variations

Try branches from a recently trimmed tree or bush, or take a few cuttings with flowers or berries from your garden.

A Screen of Wildflowers
Lilies by Candlelight

PLAYING WITH FLOWERS
—WELCOMING A GUEST—

*In one sense, all flower arrangements are gifts to be enjoyed by others, and special guests deserve
a distinctive welcome. Unique displays of flowers can guide the guest to the door or add
an extra note of elegance to the interior of the home.*

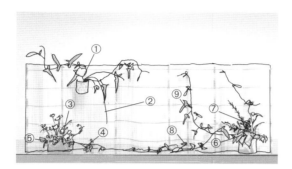

A Screen of Wildflowers

Setting

A painting-like display with bamboo mats

Materials

Early autumn grasses and wildflowers

TOP: ① Glory vine with flower   ② Long grass

BOTTOM LEFT: ③ Fleabane   ④ Clover
⑤ Bird's Foot Trefoil

RIGHT: ⑥ Day flower   ⑦ Cayratia grass
⑧ Fever vine with flowers   ⑨ Glory vine

Comments

I arranged a variety of autumn materials against a background of three bamboo mats. The mats have been set upright on an antique chest and attached to each other with fine wire.

When working with wildflowers, it is important to avoid excessive stylization or displays of technical skill, and arrange them without pretense. The flowers should give the impression that they were swept up from a field or roadside and set down here almost untouched. With the strands and shoots, you should make the most of the individual character of each plant. The finished work is quite natural, yet it also manages to suggest the highly decorative standing-screens, or *byobu*, of traditional Japanese art.

Lilies by Candlelight

Setting

A pebbled pathway

Materials

① Lily   ② Snowberry   ③ Blushing bride
④–⑤ Greenery
(④ Dwarf bamboo leaf   ⑤ Long grass)

Comments

As twilight falls, candles and fragrant lilies guide guests along the path through your garden or to your front door. Sprinkle water on the stones and they will gleam with a lustrous black hue. Pure white lilies would make a neat, simple arrangement on their own, but I went a step further and added a few rising lines of greenery. I was careful not to cover the lovely curving rim of the shell and made sure the work looked beautiful not only from all sides but from above as well.

Variations

For a charming variation, try setting a large piece of floral foam in the shell, place a candle in the center, and surround it with brilliant red and orange flowers.

PART
III

BUDS, BLOSSOMS, PETALS

1

2

3

BUDS, BLOSSOMS, PETALS

lowers unfurl their beauty in stages, but are often only appreciated at the peak of their bloom. What about the youthful promise of a bud just before it opens, or a flower's last days, when the petals flutter to the ground?

There are opportunities to create stunning arrangements at each stage in the life of a flower, whether bud, bloom, or fading. Below is a simple sequence for the miniature rose that can be adapted to almost any flower. But don't stop there. Consider, for instance, an arrangement that combines flowers in bloom with a few stray petals scattered in the foreground.

In the Bud

Setting

A side table, small nook, or quiet corner of a room

Materials

① Miniature rosebud

② Feverfew

③ Tahitian bridal veil

Comments

For the bud stage keep the vessel simple. Here, an ordinary white coffee cup works extremely well with a selection of miniature roses. I placed a loosely rolled ball of wire in the cup to secure the stems of the buds, and arranged them in a natural, casual way, emphasizing the charm of each flower's expression. Since the buds will open, consider the space between flowers and cuttings carefully. Notice how varying the lengths of the stems gives a three-dimensional feeling even in a small space like this one. I aimed for a well-balanced distribution of the different colors, and used the green, leafy material between the flowers to help fix them in position.

In Full Bloom

Setting

A corner table, shelf, or countertop

Materials

① Miniature rose, in full bloom

② Blueberry with berries

Comments

In addition to requiring more space, buds take on very different expressions when they unfold and bloom. The materials seemed somewhat crowded in one cup, so I arranged them in two, although a larger single vessel would also work. Adding fresh materials to older cuttings is a good way to accommodate the changing characteristics of the flower. As roses have a strong character I chose to combine them with unripened blueberries rather than add another type of flower. Reddish and dusted with white pollen, the berries are reminiscent of miniature roses in their bud stage.

I used a small, round needlepoint holder about one inch (two centimeters) in diameter to fix the materials in position. The longish cutting laden with fruit flows out into the surrounding space, breaking the unseen barrier between object and room, and somehow succeeds in drawing us in.

Variations

Try resting a white ceramic teacup on a pale saucer, or use a white lace cloth or doily in place of the saucer to create a graceful, European atmosphere.

Scattered Petals

Setting

A corner table or centerpiece on a large round table

Materials

① Miniature rose

② Feverfew

③ Galaxy leaf

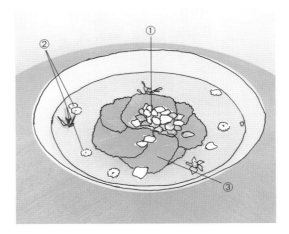

Comments

Scattered petals have a mysterious beauty, and if they are used well (which is not hard) can create a charming ambiance quite different from that of the original flowers. I used a shallow bowl, pressed the galaxy leaves into a needlepoint holder in overlapping circles, scattered the petals over a cluster of leaves, then set small flowers to float across the wide surface of the water, as if they were drifting in a quiet breeze. Viewers will enjoy watching draft in the room move the petals across the water in random patterns.

Variations

Here I used a milky white, glass container, but a transparent glass bowl would also produce a delightful effect.

A BOUQUET'S
LIFE CYCLE

1

2

3

A BOUQUET'S LIFE CYCLE

A bouquet can continue to give pleasure long after many of the original materials have faded. Save what is still fresh, try to revive what has wilted (following one or more of the procedures on pages 106 to 108), then rearrange the remaining materials in a new container.

Fragrant Gift

Materials

① Rose (two varieties)

② Globe thistle

③ Astrantia/master wort

④ Heather

⑤ Dog hobble/rainbow leaf

⑥ Sage

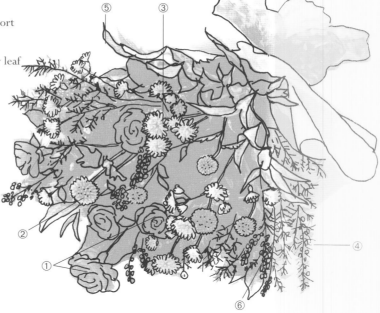

Comments

It is always a joy to give or receive flowers, and it is the thought rather than the quantity that really matters. A single rose can move the heart as much as a large bouquet. When choosing flowers for a gift, think of your feelings about the recipient, the purpose of the gift, and the person's tastes and preferences. For this bouquet, I chose roses, which have a very appealing, highly refined fragrance, as the main material, and selected other plants to complement the red and green of the roses. Avoid a monotonous impression by choosing large and small materials in a variety of shapes.

The Remains of the Bouquet: I

Materials

① Rose (two varieties) ② Globe thistle

③ Astrantia/master wort ④ Heather

⑤ Dog hobble/rainbow leaf ⑥ Sage

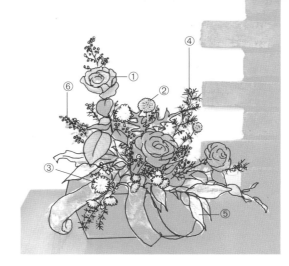

Comments

Though we are careful to change the water and take pains to preserve the freshness of the materials, flowers will eventually fade. But even when half the materials have withered, there is more than enough for another beautiful arrangement. I used a small piece of floral foam and emphasized the height of the remaining materials to make up for the loss of volume. With the same flowers but less greenery, the ribbon from the bouquet continues to complement the flowers and also serves to make up for the reduced volume of material. Trim the stems under water (page 106) to allow the clippings to draw water with renewed vigor.

Container

I selected a rather large, antique-style container with a very strong presence to add a sense of volume to the flowers. This container also beautifully underscores the deep red of the flowers.

Variations

Try arrangements in a tall, thin compote-style container or even in a silver vase or teapot. The most important thing is to express your sense of the enjoyment in arranging.

The Remains of the Bouquet: II

Materials

① Rose (two varieties)

② Globe thistle

③–④ Greenery
(③ "Moss fern" ④ Dogwood)

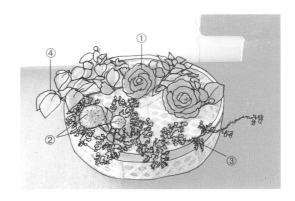

Comments

We can add a small amount of new material and continue to enjoy the beauty of the flowers by making a third arrangement. At this point, the roses have lost their leaves and they have been trimmed extensively to allow them to continue to draw water. With their shortened stems, the roses require a totally different approach. Their large, heavy petals have spread, ruling out the use of a small container, so I selected this lidded basket. I placed a water dish inside and inserted materials through openings in the woven surface, making sure that the short stems reached the water. I fleshed out the composition by adding fern and dogwood.

Variations

If you do not have a lidded basket at hand, try using a flat-bottomed basket downside up. Floating short-stemmed flowers on the surface of the water in a low, wide glass bowl or ceramic dish creates a very cool, refreshing image.

ARRANGING WITH TEACUPS

1

2

3

3

4

GLASS VESSELS
CRYSTAL CLARITY

A few small blossoms can transform a simple piece of glassware into a stylish container. The success of the arrangement will depend upon how you deal with the distinctive transparency of the glass vessel you select.

Comments

There are wine glasses or glass vessels in every home, and their beauty and unadorned simplicity make them ideal for flowers. Select your containers carefully, giving special thought to the shape and size. Consider using two or three together to compose a group arrangement—a challenging and rewarding exercise. Small, light flowers make the best materials, and a few delicate seasonal blooms are a perfect match for fragile glass containers. With tinted glass, choose materials that harmonize with the color of the container.

Method

If the glass is transparent, needlepoint holders, floral foam, or other traditional forms of support cannot be used to prop up the materials. Since the submerged stems will be visible, they must be arranged as beautifully as possible. Flowers can be supported with a single horizontal crossbar (see page 106) or by leaves or stems positioned under the water or near the surface. When using very few materials, exercise great caution in putting each individual stem in place.

Key points for each arrangement

1. Iridescence: The point here is to choose materials that harmonize with the color of the glass, so I chose flowers with color tones ranging from blue through purple. With a single crossbar to keep the materials in place, the flowers are arranged with attention to variations of shape and height. The greenery provides a sense of calm and composure. Note the clean spray of submerged stems.

2. Simple Elegance: I tried to make the most of the thin elegance of this glass. I echoed the suave vertical shape in the arrangement, extending the vertical movement and keeping the whole work crisp and clear and contained. For tall, slim containers, the materials should not be spread too widely.

3. Crystal Morning: Crystal glassware reserved for special occasions can find a new life as vessels for simple floral designs. Here, I sought to evoke the sense of purity of a bridal bouquet with this restrained arrangement in two antique wine glasses. While the materials fill the larger glass, the smaller one is only half-full, the empty space providing "breathing room" and variation.

4. Three Small Graces: I lined up three glasses on a railing and created simple arrangements with flowers cut very short. The challenge for this type of arrangement is to create variations among the three mini-compositions while producing an overall sense of harmony.

Iridescence

1

Materials

① Joe-pye weed ② Delphinium
③ Swan River daisy ④ Rosemary

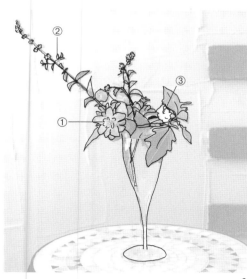

Simple Elegance

2

Materials

① Hidden lily ② Peppermint ③ Gooseberry

Crystal Morning

3

Materials

LARGE GLASS

① Begonia ② Wax flower ③ Knotgrass
④ Long grass

SMALL GLASS

⑤ Geranium ⑥ Pink ⑦ Long grass

Three Small Graces

4

Materials

LEFT

① Tobacco plant ② Meadow rue ③ Star jasmine leaf

CENTER

④ Fire lily ⑤ Yam leaf

RIGHT

⑥ Spotted campanula ⑦ Meadow rue ⑧ Star jasmine leaf

SIMPLE TECHNIQUES

Buying & Caring for Materials

When buying materials, it is important to keep in mind that cut flowers are highly susceptible to wind and heat. Flowers kept in refrigerated glass cases may look very presentable but they can bloom or wilt in a short time when suddenly removed and exposed to a warmer environment. When you bring them home, trim their stems under water or use one of the other methods introduced in the following pages to preserve their freshness. Store them at room temperature, keep them out of direct sunlight and away from open windows or drafts, and do not handle them too much since any heat—including the warmth given off by your hands—can harm them. This is particularly true of such frail specimens as poppies and wildflowers. When cutting flowers from your garden, gather them in the morning, particularly in summer. Heat is their worst enemy.

Fill vases of arranged flowers with plenty of water and change the water or add to it daily. It is best to display flowers in a place where the temperature is relatively low and the humidity is high. In an air-conditioned room where the air is dry, spray the arrangement with water, especially the underside of the leaves. As time passes and the flowers lose their vitality, remove them from the container, wrap them in damp sheets of newspaper, trim the stems under water, and let them stand in deep water until they revive (see method 4 on page 107). Before rearranging them, wash the container thoroughly to remove any fungus or bacteria.

Selecting a Container

The true beauty of arranged flowers only emerges when the materials and the vessel merge in a unified work of art. Therefore, do not think of the container and the arrangement separately, but treat the vase as another element of the display, like the flowers, leaves, and branches. Whether the container is made of clay, glass, bamboo, wood, or metal there is enormous variation within each category. Ceramic vessels, for instance, range from the heavy, earthy quality of folk pottery to delicate, finely painted works of porcelain. When selecting a container, consider the color, design, and shape first, then the overall character of the piece.

As a general rule, a somewhat narrow range of flowers will look good in containers with bold designs or with extremely novel or unconventional shapes, whereas plain vessels or those with subdued colors and subtle designs are much more versatile. A second general principal to bear in mind is that light-colored vases appear larger than those with deep, dark colors.

The setting and the quantity of materials are essential factors in determining the size and position of the container. Before composing your arrangement, consider the overall space and (1) whether the size of the flower vessel is appropriate for the space and (2) whether the vessel should be set in the center or to one side, taking into account the position of the viewers and the direction the materials will be facing.

Baskets and other containers fashioned from natural materials make ideal receptacles for flowers and have a number of advantages. They are light, come in many colors, shapes, and sizes, and do not break even when dropped. Bamboo, willow, and wisteria baskets are the most adaptable. To use them, simply place an inconspicuous container inside the basket to hold water and your arrangement.

In addition to the obvious choices, keep in mind that almost anything can be a stage for flowers. Try using coffee cups, teacups, dishes, kitchen bowls, and spice containers. Look around your house and you will be surprised at how many familiar objects you can enlist as containers for floral displays.

Combining & Arranging Materials

Like containers, flowers come in all shapes, sizes, and colors, and each has its own unique character. There are lovely, soft wildflowers and strong, brilliantly colored cultivated breeds. No matter which flowers you select, try to combine them with other materials in a harmonious manner, drawing out the most beautiful and expressive aspect of each individual flower. It is important to think in terms of both major and minor materials, and to create gradations in the green foliage. While all elements are important, begin by deciding what is to be the main point or subject of your display, then arrange other flowers, branches, and leaves to create a setting for that subject.

Greater skill and judgment will come naturally with increased experience. This is true particularly about the amount of material to use and what to cut away. Always avoid a heavy, crowded look. Try to think of "empty space" as a vital, living part of your composition, as important as the flowers, branches, and container. Consider the upper and lower, left and right sides of the work, which should be balanced but not symmetrical. Remember that an arrangement with a simple symmetrical balance is easily absorbed by the viewer and soon becomes monotonous and predictable.

If there is one critical part of any arrangement, it is the base—the area where the materials enter the vessel. This area should be neat and concentrated. No matter how beautiful the upper part of the work may be, if the base is too wide or sloppy, the arrangement will look weak and lack focus.

Finally, there are flowers like roses and gerberas that you can obtain all year long, but seasonal flowers are far more intriguing, and when arranged together these perishable gifts from nature always make the best and most rewarding combinations.

Basic Tools & Support Techniques

Cutting Tools

There are a number of simple tools that you should have on hand when arranging. To cut materials, you will need a scissors or a knife. Choose a pair of scissors that is easy for you to hold and that will not rust easily. Sharpness is essential since dull blades can damage stems and branches, reducing their ability to absorb water and thus retarding their freshness and vitality. Since scissors also become dull when you cut floral wire and tape, keep a second pair close by. A pair of small garden shears can be helpful in cutting thick branches and stems (although I did not rely on them much for the arrangements in this book).

Knives do not damage plant cells as much as scissors do, so use them when either will work. It is also possible to cut stems on a greater angle with a knife than with scissors. A larger-angled cut exposes more surface area, allowing the plant to absorb more water. Though knives are not as good as scissors for cutting small stems and flowers, they are useful for cutting floral foam, which is used to hold the materials in place in some arrangements.

   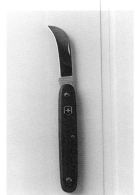

house scissors   ikebana scissors   garden scissors   kitchen knife

Needlepoint Holder

These holders have a field of fine pins that allow you to firmly anchor flowers and other plant material in place. They are particularly useful in securing the positions of bulkier cuttings such as small branches and top-heavy cuttings, and are indispensable for keeping materials tight and centered in wide-mouthed and shallow containers. Needlepoint holders are sturdy and stable and come in a variety of sizes.

Floral Foam

A hard green spongelike material, floral foam is inexpensive, easy to use, and can be found in most craft shops. Since stems and thin branches may be inserted at any angle, floral foam works for a wide variety of arrangements. Do not use foam for groupings with thick branches or heavy stems.

To use, cut off the portion you need with a knife and place it in a bucket filled with water. The foam will absorb the water naturally as it sinks to the bottom. After it has sunk, it is ready for use. Do not force it into the water or pour water over it. Floral foam is a synthetic material and holes cannot be repaired. Use it once and then discard it.

Floral Tape and Plastic Pin Holder

Floral tape, a type of malleable rubber tape, is also referred to as "floral clay," "decorator adhesive," or simple "adhesive tape." Separately or in tandem with a plastic pin holder, it is used to secure floral foam in place. The tape is attached to the inside surface of the container, and the pin holder (also know as a "frog") is fixed to the tape, then the floral foam is pressed into the points of the pin holder. Frogs can also

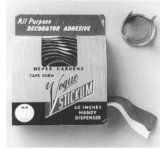

be used to fix foam in a very wide, shallow dish or container where the vessel's edge is too low to provide support for the flowers. The sink arrangement on page 39 shows how the three can be used together for unique situations.

Wire

Both thin and thick wire are used for flower arrangements. Thin wire can be used to make wreaths and tie ribbons, or even to secure a container in place when it rests on a narrow space or rough surface.

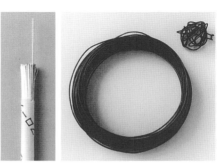

Traditionally, in Japan, thicker wire served to train the branches of bonsai. Here, it is rolled in a loose ball, placed in containers, then stems and branches are inserted in the spaces between the rolled wire, adjusting the wire as necessary.

Twig Crosspieces

Single crossbars or two bars placed one above the other in the shape of a cross can be set near the lip of a container to secure plant material in the desired position or angle. Cut a twig(s) to the diameter of the container's mouth and wedge it securely in the opening slightly below the rim. This method works particularly well with cylindrical containers. The crosspiece(s) should be invisible in the completed arrangement.

Preservation Methods for Plant Materials

Before you begin an arrangement, you will need to cut the stems of all your materials to allow them to draw and retain water, which will help preserve the freshness of your display. While the appropriate method depends on the species, size, and condition of the plants, begin with method 1, which is sufficient for most flowers. *And remember that it is important to cut the stems off beneath the surface of the water.* When you are unsure of which method to use, work in descending order. Try cutting under water with a scissors first (method 1). If your material does not hold up in the arrangement, or wilts soon after, try cutting it under water with a knife (method 2). And it never hurts to set the trimmed material in deep water for a few hours (method 4), or until you are ready to begin.

1. Cutting under water with a scissors

EXAMPLE: Most flowers

This is the easiest and most common method. Just place the base of the stem under water and cut about 1 inch (2 centimeters) off *at an angle*. To increase the effectiveness of this method, cut the stem in deep water to take advantage of the increased water pressure, which assists the stem's ability to draw in liquid. This method works best with flowers. Ideally, you should trim the stems every day.

2. Cutting under water with a knife

EXAMPLES: *Sunflower*
Denphale
Fern shoot
Lily

3. Bending & breaking

EXAMPLES: *Chrysanthemum*
Prairie gentian
Carnation
Pink

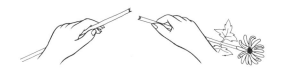

If the flowers begin to wilt soon after they are cut, try trimming their stems with a knife, which causes less damage to the stem. For materials with thicker stems, try bending and breaking the stem. Check the sample flower list under each heading to determine which method is best.

4. Placing in deep water

EXAMPLES: *Calla lily*
Narcissus
Gerbera

For drooping or wilted flowers or stems, where simply cutting under water is not sufficient, wrap the plants in newspaper, cut under water, and leave in deep water for one or two hours.

5. Placing in boiling water

EXAMPLES: *Pampas grass*
Plumed thistle
Spindle tree
Hydrangea

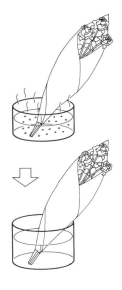

Wrap the plants in newspaper, leaving the base of the stems exposed. Place the exposed area in boiling water for about three minutes, then quickly transfer to a bucket of cold water for one to two hours. This method shocks the plants into drawing water and is most effective for cuttings that draw water with difficulty. The paper, which soon becomes saturated, draws water to other parts of the plants.

6. *Charring the base of the stems*

EXAMPLES: Rose
Master wort
Southern star
Some wildflowers

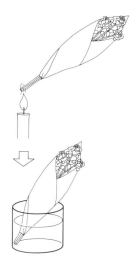

Char the cut ends of the stems for about 30 seconds with the flame of a lighter, gas burner, or candle until the surface is blackened, then place them immediately in a bucket of cold water. When charring the materials, be careful to protect the leaves and flowers from heat by wrapping everything but the base of the stem in newspaper. Since the charring increases the ability of each cutting to absorb water, do not cut off the charred portion of the stem.

7. *Crushing the stem*

EXAMPLES: Thunberg spirea
Dogwood

Use a wooden hammer to crush 2 to 4 inches (5 to 10 centimeters) of a thick stem or hard branch in order to increase the area that can absorb water. After crushing, quickly place the stem in deep water. Crush but do not pulverize the stems. This technique works best with branches and tree materials.

8. *Splitting or scraping branches*

SPLITTING: Dogwood   SCRAPING: Cypress
Willow   Rosemary
Pine

With thick or hard branches, cutting the base in a cross pattern or scraping off the bark around the base will increase its ability to absorb water. Work carefully and use sharp tools to avoid excessive damage to plant cells.

9. *Combining techniques*

In some cases, a combination of methods works best. You could use 3 & 6, 3 & 5, or 6 & 4. In more difficult cases combining three different techniques can be effective: you might start with 7 (or 8) and then move on to 6 & 4. As your experience grows you will soon learn which plants flourish under each type of treatment.

LIST OF FLOWERS BY ARRANGEMENT

*S*ince an exact English equivalent was unavailable for many of the plants indigenous to Japan, I have listed the Latin and Japanese names here for the curious reader and the botanically inclined. However, keep in mind that it is far better to follow the spirit of the arrangement, choosing flowers and plant cuttings from your area, than to try to replicate the exact selection. In the list below, the scientific and Japanese names follow the English common name.

Wildflowers in Glass—PAGE 10

1 Astrantia/master wort • Astrantia major • Astrantia major
2 Meadow rue • Thalictrum sp. • Karamatsu-so
3 Purple wildflower • Stachys japonica v. intermedia • Inu-goma
4 Evergreen fern • Davalia mariesii Moore • Shinobu

Iris Centerpiece—PAGES 10–11

1 Rabbit-ear iris • Iris laevigata • Kakitsubata
2 Dogwood • Cornus kousa • Yamaboushi
3 Bulrush/zebra Bulrush • Scirpus tabernaemontani f. pictus • Shima-futoi

Hydrangea & Willow—PAGE 14

1 Pyramid hydrangea • Hydrangea paniculata f. grandiflora • Pyramid ajisai (Minazuki)
2 Dragon willow • Salix matsudana v. tortuosa • Unryu-yanagi

Flowers in Tandem—PAGE 15, TOP

BOTTLE

1 Flowering indigo • Polygonum tinectorium • Ai
2 Spindle tree (sprig) • Euonymus sieboldianus • Mayumi
3 Carex grass • Carex sp. • Wabi-suge

CUP

4 Toad lily • Tricyrtis cv. kohaku • Hototogisu

Table Centerpiece in Natural Tones—PAGE 15, BOTTOM

1 Beauty berry • Callicarpa dichotoma • Komurasaki
2 Vine carrot (with flowers) • Codonopsis lanceolata • Tsuru-ninjin
3 Evergreen fern • Onychium japonicum • Tachi-shinobu

Spring Nouveau—PAGE 18

1 "Fried egg" • Limnanthes douglasii • Fried egg
2 False indigo • Baptisia australis • Murasaki-sendai-hagi
3 Quaking grass • Briza maxima • Koban-so

Flowers & Berries on a Tray—PAGE 19, TOP

1 Cornflower • Rudbeckia sp. • Rudbeckia
2 Grapevine (with unripe grapes) • Ampelopsis Brevipedunculata • No-budou

Vase of Autumn Colors—PAGE 19, BOTTOM

1 Calla lily • Zantedeschia sp. • Calla
2 "Chocolate" cosmos • Cosmos atrosanguineus • Chocolate cosmos
3 Asparagus fern • Asparagus scandens • Asparagus
4 Evergreen fern • Onychium japonicum • Tachi-shinobu

Through Glass, Brightly—PAGE 22

LEFT

1 Red clover • Trifolium repens (pratense) • Murasaki-tsumekusa
2 Asparagus fern • Asparagus macowanii • Asparagus
3 "Moss fern" • Selaginella remotifolia ssp. • Kurama-goke
4 Greenery • Eleocharis parvinux • Kotsubu-numa-hari-i

RIGHT

5 Clematis • Clematis Durandii • Durandii (Bell tessen)
6 Balloon vine • Cardiospermum halicacabum. • Fusen-kazura
7 Foxtail • Setaria sp. • Enokoro-gusa
8 Greenery • Cyperus involucratus • Cyperus

Cornflowers in Bamboo—PAGE 23

1 Cornflower • Centaurea cyanus • Yaguruma-so
2 Mini freesia • Freesia cv. Eckl • Mini freesia
3 Green bell • Silene vulgaris • Green bell

Harbinger of Spring—PAGE 26

1 Cherry blossom • Prunus subhirtella Mig. • Higan-zakura
2 Tulip • Tulipa cv. • Tulip

Invitation to a Moon-viewing Party—PAGE 27, TOP

1 Pampas grass • Miscanthus sinensis cv. Zebrinus • Takanoha-susuki
2 Boneset/thoroughwort • Eupatorium japonicum • Fuji-bakama
3 Burnet • Sanguisorba officinalis • Waremoko

Orchids & Burnished Wood—PAGE 27, BOTTOM

1 Orchid • Dendrobium bigibbum ssp. • Denphale
2 Viburnum (with berries) • Viburnum tinnus • Viburnum tinnus

Tropical Fruits & Flowers—PAGE 30
1 Mini-pineapple • Ananas nanus • Mini-pineapple
2 Blueberry • Vaccinium corymbosum • Blueberry
2 Cherry • Prunus avium • Sakuranbo
3 English ivy • Hedera helix • Ivy
4 Coral bells • Heuchera sanguinea • Tsubo-sango

Mini-Bouquet of Herbs—PAGE 31
1 Dark opal basil • Ocimum basilicum cv. • Dark opal basil
2 Peppermint • Mentha piperita • Peppermint
3 Rosemary • Rosmarinus officinalis • Rosemary
4 Creeping thyme • Thymus serpyllum • Creeping thyme
5 Dusty miller • Senecio bicolor • Shirotae-giku

Flowers & Herbs in a Seashell—PAGE 34, TOP
1 American blue • Evolvulus nuthallenus • American blue
2 Dusty miller • Senecio bicolor • Shirotae-giku
3 Spearmint • Mentha spicata cv. • Spearmint
4 Lavender cotton • Santolina sp. • Santolina gray
5 English ivy • Hedera helix • Ivy

Elegant Porcelain—PAGE 34, BOTTOM
1 Bleeding heart • Dicentra spectabilis • Taitsuri-so (Keman-so)
2 Columbine • Aquilegia flabellata • Odamaki

Herbs & Shimmering Silver—PAGE 35
1 Lavender • Lavandula stoechas • French lavender
2 Curry plant • Helichrysum angustifolium • Curry plant
3 Lavender cotton • Santolina sp. • Santolina gray
4 Spearmint • Mentha spicata cv. • Spearmint
5 Thyme • Thymus vulgaris • Thyme
6 English ivy • Hedera helix • Ivy

A Horizontal Display—PAGE 38, TOP
1 Miniature rose • Rosa hybrida cv. • Mini-bara
2 Peppermint • Mentha piperita • Peppermint
3 Stemona • Stemona japonica • Rikyu-so

Simple Greenery—PAGE 38, BOTTOM
1 Spider plant • Chlorophytum comosum • Orizuru-ran
2 Isotoma • Isotoma axillaris • Isotoma
3 Broom • Cytisus scoparius cv. • Enishida
4 Fennel • Foeniculum vulgare • Fennel

Bathroom Bouquet—PAGE 39
1 Rose • Rosa hybrida cv. • Bara
2 Small sunflower • Helianthus debilis cv. • Mini-himawari
3 Smoke tree • Cotinus coggygria • Smoke tree
4 Rosemary • Rosmarinus officinalis • Rosemary

Bedside Bouquet—PAGE 42
1 Lapeirousia • Lapeirousia laxa • Lapeirousia (Hime-hiougi)
2 Buttercup • Ranunculus silerifolius • Kitsune-no-botan
3 Euonymus • Euonymus radicans • Tsuru-masaki

Angel's Wreath—PAGE 43, TOP
1 Miniature Rose • Rosa hybrida cv. • Mini-bara
2 Kiwi vine • Actinidia chinensis • Kiwi
3 Spearmint • Mentha spicata cv. • Spearmint
4 Silver brunia • Brunia laevis • Silver brunia
5 English ivy • Hedera helix • Ivy

Breaking with Form—PAGE 43, BOTTOM
1 Amsonia • Amsonia elliptica • Choji-so
2 Meadowsweet • Gillenia trifoliata • Mitsuba-shimotsuke
3 Winter hazel • Corylopsis pauciflora • Hyuga-mizuki

In a Looking Glass—PAGE 46
1 Tulip • Tulipa cv. • Tulip
2 Adonis • Adonis aestivalis • Adonis (Natsuzaki-fukuju-so)
3 Kalanchoe • Kalanchoe millabera. • Kalanchoe millabera

Lively Corner—PAGE 47, LEFT
1 Thistle • Cirsium japonicum • No-azami
2 Ruby grass • Rhynchelytrum repens • Ruby grass
3 Blueberry • Vaccinium corymbosum • Blueberry

Spring Visitors—PAGE 47, RIGHT
1 Amur adonis • Adonis amurensis • Fukuju-so
2 Fern shoot • Osmunda japonica • Hime-zenmai
3 Green barley • Triticum aestivum • Mugi

Filling a Niche—PAGE 50, LEFT
1 Green brier (with berries) • Smilax china • Sankirai
2 Orchid • Ascocentrum x Vanda cv. • Ascocenda Mokara
3 Rosemary • Rosmarinus officinalis • Rosemary
4 Lawson cypress • Chamaecyparis obtusa • Kujaku-hiba

Around a Stairway—PAGES 50–51
1 Bletilla • Bletilla striata • Shi-ran
2 False goat's beard • Astilbe arendsii • Astilbe
3 Glossy abelia • Abelia grandiflora • Abelia (Hanazono-tsukubane-utsugi)

Green Cascade—PAGE 51, RIGHT
1 Periwinkle • Vinca minor • Tsuru-nichinichi-so
2 Clematis • Clematis texensis • Clematis
3 Cascading greenery • Cynodon dactylon • Gyogi-shiba
4 False anemone • Anemonopsis macrophylla • Renge-shoma
5 Agrimony • Agrimonia pilosa v. japonica • Kin-mizuhiki
6 Lotus (leaf) • Nelumbo nucfera • Hasu

Hearth-Side Flowers—PAGE 54
1 Glove tulip • Calachortus cv. Pursh • Calachortus
2 Thunberg spirea • Spiraea thunbergii • Yukiyanagi
3 Kohuhu • Pittosporum tenuifolium • Pittosporum
4 Lady's mantle • Alchemilla mollis • Alchemilla mollis

Folk Craft Elegance—PAGE 55

1 Cherry sage • Salvia michrophlla • Cherry sage
2 Spearmint • Mentha spicata cv. • Spearmint
3 English ivy • Hedera helix • Ivy
4 Pink-tingled leaf • Chenopodium album v. centrorubrun • Akaza

Christmas Centerpiece—PAGE 58

1 Oregon fir • Abies sp. • Momi
2 Southern star • Oxypetalum caeruleum • White star
3 Miniature rose • Rosa hybrida cv. • Mini-bara
4 Cape myrtle • Filica pubscens • Phylica

A Window Scene—PAGE 59, TOP

1 Miniature rose (yellow & red) • Rosa hybrida cv. • Mini-bara
2 Lawson cypress • Chamaecyparis obtusa cv. • Kujaku-hiba

A Different Kind of Wreath—PAGE 59, BOTTOM

1 Rose • Rosa hybrida cv. • Bara
2 Kiwi vine • Actinidia chinensis • Kiwi
3 Leucadendron • Leucadendron sp. • Leucadendron
4 Dusty miller • Senecio bicolor • Shirotae-giku
5 Grain stalk • Calamagrostis arundiuacea • Nogariyasu
6 Dog hobble/rainbow leaf • Leucothoe walteri cv. "Rainbow" • Rainbow leaf
7 Gum tree • Eucalyptus sp. • Yukari
8 English ivy • Hedera helix • Ivy

Picnic Flowers—PAGE 62

1 Small sunflower • Helianthus debilis • Mini-himawari
2 Violet foxtail • Setaria viridis f. misera • Murasaki-enokoro-gusa
3 Umbrella fern • Dicranopteris linearis • Shida
4 Begonia (leaf) • Begonia grandiss ssp. • Shukaido

Welcoming Guests—PAGE 63, TOP

1 Yellow cosmos • Cosmos sulphureus • Kibana-kosumusu
2 Monkshood • Aconitum sp. • Torikabuto
3 Themeda grass • Themeda triandra • Karu-kaya
4 Japanese honeysuckle • Lonicera japonica • Suikazura
5 Umbrella plant • Cyperus amuricus • Cha-gayatsuri

Borrowing Background—PAGE 63, BOTTOM

1 Japanese rose of Sharon • Hibisucus sp. • Yahazu-bonten-bana
2 Viburnum • Viburnum opulus cv. Compactum • Compact berry
3 Knotgrass • Polygonum filiforme • Mizuhiki

A Romantic Evening—PAGE 66

1 Tulip • Tulipa cv. • Tulip
2 Lily of the valley • Convallaria majais • Suzuran
3 Fairy bells • Melasphaerula ramosa • Melasphelder
4 Acacia • Acacia sp. • Mimoza

An Afternoon Tête-à-Tête—PAGE 67

1 Marguerite • Chrysanthemum cv. "Wedding" • Wedding marguerite
2 Delphinium • Delphinium × belladonna • Delphinium bella-donna
3 Corn lily • Ixia sp. • Ixia blue
4 Small lily (leaf) • Disporum sessile • Houchaku-so

Approaching Ikebana—PAGE 70

1 Amaryllis • Hippeastrum hybrida cv. • Amaryllis
2 Bittersweet (with berries) • Celastrus orbiculatus • Tsuru-ume-modoki
3 Knotweed/jointweed • Polygonum cuspidatum • Itadori
4 Knotgrass • Polygonum filiforme • Mizuhiki

A Touch of Lacquer—PAGE 71, TOP

1 Black lily • Fritillaria camtschatcensis • Kuro-yuri
2 Cymbidium • Cymbidium goeringii • Shun-ran

Welcoming the New Year—PAGE 71, BOTTOM

1 Camellia • Camellia japonica • Tsubaki
2 Japanese black Pine • Pinus thunbergii. • Kuro-matsu
3 Willow (with leaf buds) • Salix koriyanagi • Kori-yanagi

Three Round Tables—PAGE 74

LEFT

1 Aster • Aster ageratoides ssp. • Nokon-giku
2 "Wild frosty" • Keisukea japonica • Shimobashira

CENTER

3 Clematis • Clematis Durandii • Durandii (Bell tessen)
4 Blueberry (leaf) • Vaccinium corymbosum • Blueberry

RIGHT

5 Rose • Rosa hybrida cv. • Bara
6 Clematis (with seed) • Clematis hybrida cv. • Clematis

Drinks & Hors d'Oeuvres—PAGE 75

FRONT

1 Aster • Aster novi-belgii • Yuzen-giku
2 Toad lily (pink) • Tricyrtis formosana • hototogisu
3 Leaves to cover • Cryptotaenia canadensis ssp. • Murasaki-mitsuba

BACK

4 Persimmon branch (with unripe fruit) • Diospyros kaki • Roua-gaki
5 Toad lily (yellow) • Tricyrtis latifolia • Tamagawa-hototogisu
6 Sweet scabious • Scabiosa japonica • Matsumushi-so
7 Leaves to cover • Cryptotaenia canadensis ssp. • Murasaki-mitsuba

Unexpected Encounter—PAGE 78

1 Spray chrysanthemum • Chrysanthemum morifolium • Spray-giku
2 Corn cockle • Agrostemma githago • Agrostemma (Mugi-nadeshiko)
3 Gentian • Gentiana scaba v. buergeri • Rindou
4 Millet • Setaria italica • Awa
5 Laurel • Danae racemosa • Italian ruscus

Silk & Flowers——PAGE 79, TOP

1 Prairie gentian • Eustoma grandiflorum cv. • Toruko-kikyo

2 China aster • Callistephus chinensis cv. • Aster

3 Stemona • Stemona japonica • Rikyu-so

Bamboo Forest——PAGE 79, BOTTOM

1 Hydrangea • Hydrangea macrophylla • Ajisai

2 Horse mint • Monarda punctata • Monarda punctata

3 Smoke grass • Panicum capillare • Smoke grass

4 Ground cover • Bryophyta • Koke

A Screen of Wildflowers——PAGE 82

TOP

1 Glory vine (with flower) • Calystegia hederacea • Ko-hirugao

2 Long grass • Carex nanella • Hosoba-hikage-suge

BOTTOM LEFT

3 Fleabane • Erigeron annuusus • Hime-joon

4 Clover • Trifolium dubium • Kometsubu-tsumekusa

5 Bird's Foot Trefoil • Lotus corniculatus • Miyako-gusa

RIGHT

6 Day flower • Commelina communis • Tsuyukusa

7 Cayratia grass • Cayratia japonica • Yabu-garashi

8 Fever vine (with flowers) • Paederia scandens • Hekuso-kazura

9 Glory vine • Calystegia hederacea • Ko-hirugao

Lilies by Candlelight——PAGE 83

1 Lily • Lilium cv. • Yuri

2 Snowberry • Symphoricarpos albus • Symphoricarpos

3 Blushing bride • Serruria florida • Serruiria

4 Dwarf bamboo (leaf) • Sasa sp. • Sasa

5 Long grass/ophiopogon grass • Ophiopogon japonicus • Ryu-no-hige

In the Bud——PAGE 86

1 Miniature rosebud • Rosa hybrida cv. • Mini-bara

2 Feverfew • Chrysanthemum parthenium • Matricaria (Natsu-shiro-giku)

3 Tahitian bridal veil • Gibasis pellucida • Bridal veil

In Full Bloom——PAGE 87, TOP

1 Miniature rose, in full bloom • Rosa hybrida cv. • Mini-bara

2 Blueberry (with berries) • Vaccinium corymbosum. • Blueberry

Scattered Petals——PAGE 87, BOTTOM

1 Miniature rose • Rosa hybrida cv. • Mini-bara

2 Feverfew • Chrysanthemum parthenium • Matricaria (Natsu-shiro-giku)

3 Galaxy (leaf) • Galax urceolata • Galax

Fragrant Gift——PAGE 90

1 Rose (two varieties) • Rosa hybrida cv. • Bara

2 Globe thistle • Echinops ritro • Ruri-tama-azami

3 Astrantia/master wort • Astrantia major • Astrantia major

4 Heather • Erica • Erica

5 Dog hobble/rainbow leaf • Leucothoe walteri cv. "Rainbow" • Rainbow leaf

6 Sage • Salvia prumosa • Salvia prumosa

The Remains of the Bouquet I——PAGE 91, TOP

1 Rose (two varieties) • Rosa hybrida cv. • Bara

2 Globe thistle • Echinops ritro • Ruri-tama-azami

3 Astrantia/master wort • Astrantia major • Astrantia major

4 Heather • Erica • Erica

5 Dog hobble/rainbow leaf • Leucothoe walteri cv. "Rainbow" • Rainbow leaf

6 Sage • Salvia prumosa • Salvia prumosa

The Remains of the Bouquet II——PAGE 91, BOTTOM

1 Rose (two varieties) • Rosa hybrida cv. • Bara

2 Globe thistle • Echinops ritro • Ruri-tama-azami

3 "Moss fern" • Salaginella remotifolia ssp. • Kurama-goke

4 Dogwood • Cornus kousa • Yamaboushi

Leaves and Berries——PAGE 94, LEFT

1 Black berries • Liriope platyphylla • Yabu-ran

2 Dusty miller • Senecio bicolor • Shirotae-giku

3 Cowslip • Lachenalia cv. • Lachenalia veridiflora

4 Lavender • Lavandula stoechas • French lavender

Coffee Cup Creation——PAGE 94, TOP RIGHT

1 Coneflower • Rudbeckia sp. • Rudbeckia

2 Lantana (two colors, with seeds) • Lantana camara • Lantana

Purple Wildflowers——PAGE 94, BOTTOM

1 Plantain lily • Hosta lancifolia • Koba-giboushi

2 Toad lily • Tricyrtis hirta • Hototogisu

3 Floss flower • Ageratum houstonianum • Ageratum

4 Thunberg geranium (leaf) • Geranium thunbergii • Gen-no-shoko

In a Japanese Teacup——PAGE 95, TOP

1 Sweet scabious • Scabiosa japonica • Matsumushi-so

2 Sea holly • Eryngium sp. • Eryngium

3 "Antenna" flower • Atractylodes japonica • Okera

4 Plantain lily (leaf) • Hosta lancifolia • Koba-giboushi

Autumn Breakfast——PAGE 95, BOTTOM

1 "Hatbox" flower • Abutilon theophrasti • Asa-no-mi (Ichibi)

2 Sneezeweed • Helinium autumnale • Helinium

3 Hare's ear • Bupleurum falcatum • Mishima-saiko

4 Euphorbia • Euphorbia robbiae • Euphorbia

5 Wax tree (leaf) • Rhus succedanea • Hazenoki

6 Wildflower vine • Amphicarpaea edgeworthii v. japonica • Yabu-mame

Iridescence——PAGE 98, TOP

1 Joe-pye weed • Eupatorium sp. • Eupatorium

2 Delphinium • Delphinium cv. • Delphinium

3 Swan River daisy • Brachycome iberidifolia • Swan River

4 Rosemary • Rosmarinus officinalis • Rosemary

Simple Elegance—PAGE 98, BOTTOM

1 Hidden lily • Curcuma sp. • Mini curcuma

2 Peppermint • Mentha piperita cv. "Citrata"
   • Au de cologne mint/peppermint

3 Gooseberry • Physalis sp. • Star train

Crystal Morning—PAGE 99, TOP

LARGE

1 Begonia • Begonia grandis ssp. • Shukaido

2 Wax flower • Chamelaucium uncinatum • Wax flower

3 Knotgrass • Polygonum filiforme • Mizuhiki

4 Long grass/ophiopogon grass • Ophiopogon japonicus
   • Ryu-no-hige

SMALL

5 Geranium • Pelargonium cv. • Geranium

6 Pink • Dianthus sp. • Summer lavender

7 Long grass/ophiopogon grass • Ophiopogon japonicus
   • Ryu-no-hige

Three Small Graces—PAGE 99, BOTTOM

LEFT

1 Tobacco plant • Nicotiana alata • Hana-tabako

2 Meadow rue • Thalictrum sp. • Karamatsu-so

3 Star jasmine (leaf) • Trachelospermum asiaticum
   • Goshiki-zuta (Teika-kazura)

CENTER

4 Fire lily • Lycoris sp. • Lycoris

5 Yam (leaf) • Dioscorea japonica • Yama-no-imo

RIGHT

6 Spotted campanula • Campanula punctata • Hotaru-bukuro

7 Meadow rue • Thalictrum sp. • Karamatsu-so

8 Star jasmine (leaf) • Trachelospermum asiaticum
   • Goshiki-zuta (Teika-kazura)

INDEX